MASTERPIECES OF
PAINTING AND SCULPTURE

from

The Detroit Institute of Arts

DETROIT - 1949

Cover
THE ARCHDUKE FERDINAND AT THE BATTLE OF NORDLINGEN
PETER PAUL RUBENS, *Flemish* (1577-1640)
GIFT OF THE RALPH HARMAN BOOTH FUND

MADAME HENRIETTE DE FRANCE AS A VESTAL VIRGIN
JEAN MARC NATTIER, *French (1685-1766)*
GIFT OF MR. AND MRS. EDGAR B. WHITCOMB

TABLE OF CONTENTS

Explanatory Note: In sizes height always precedes width; when only one size is given, it refers to the height of the object illustrated.

THE AIM of the Detroit Institute of Arts
is to represent within one building, in a single, clear, organic sequence,
the whole story of the arts in human society. The collection begins with the
first appearance of the instinct of design in the flints of prehistoric man
and traces its development through every important stage of art down to
the present day. Each stage is represented by a gallery which aims to
illustrate, by carefully chosen examples, the culture of a single age as it was
expressed by the arts. In consequence all the different media of art are
shown together—painting, sculpture, furniture, metal work, glass, enamels,
whatever else may be an important form of art in that age being grouped
together as the organic expression of a period of life. The arts of the more
distant past are installed in architectural settings which, though modern,
endeavor to suggest the original setting in scale, color and decoration.

The purpose of this book of illustrations is to offer a convenient
souvenir of the range and quality of the collections, so far as they are
formed by paintings and sculpture. It serves also as a companion volume
to the *Catalogue of Paintings,* of which the latest edition appeared in 1944.
Our hope is that it will serve the visitor as a pleasant reminder of our
museum and aid him to form a lasting acquaintance with the great works
of art which are housed here.

The city of Detroit, founded by French settlers from the lower St.
Lawrence in 1701, has twice begun its life over again. A great fire in
1805 wiped out the entire eighteenth century French village. The American
city which grew up in the nineteenth century was known for its beauty and
for the leisurely charm of its life, whose tempo was inherited to some
degree from the old French settlement. The rise of the automobile industry
at the beginning of the twentieth century again almost completely wiped
out the nineteenth century city and produced the great industrial, engi-
neering and technological metropolis of today.

The art museum was founded as a private corporation in 1885 and grew slowly but steadily until it was taken over as a branch of the city government in 1919. Since then it has functioned under the direction of an Arts Commission appointed by the mayor of Detroit. The old private corporation has, however, remained in being, to act as a sustaining society whose memberships and income from endowments are used to add to the collections of the Institute. Citizens of Detroit and friends of this community, by membership in the Detroit Museum of Art Founders Society, as it is now called, and by their donations, have made it possible for the museum to grow to its present stature. The Art Institute is thus sustained by a partnership of public ownership and private support, working together in a different form than in any other American art museum.

E. P. RICHARDSON

HEAD OF A MAN. From Tell el-Amarna. New Kingdom, Eighteenth Dynasty, Reign of Amenhotep III (about 1411-1375 B.C.). Limestone, 4 inches. Acc. no. 46.57. Gift of the Founders Society, 1946.

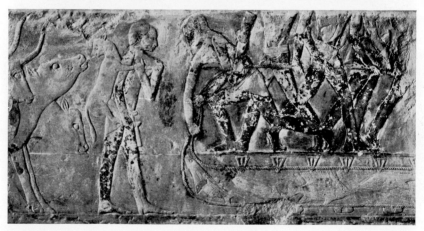

PEASANTS DRIVING CATTLE AND FISHING. From Saqqara. Old
Kingdom, Fifth Dynasty (about 2560-2420 B.C.). Painted limestone,
32 x 18 inches and 27 x 18½ inches. Acc. no. 30.371. City appropriation,
1930.

HEAD OF A KING. New Kingdom, Eighteenth to Twentieth Dynasty
(about *1580-1085* B.C.). Rose granite, 19¼ x 22⅜ inches. Acc. no. 31.73.
Gift of Mrs. Lillian Henkel Haass and Mrs. Trent McMath, 1931.

FIGURE OF A MAN. From Bismaya (Adab). Reign of Lugal-kisal-si of
Uruk (about 2700 B.C.). Limestone, 14⅛ inches. Acc. no. 44.78. Gift of
the Sarah Bacon Hill Fund, 1944.

EAGLE-HEADED WINGED BEING POLLINATING THE SACRED
TREE. From the palace of Assur-nazir-pal, Nimrud (Calah). Reign of
Assur-nazir-pal (885-860 B.C.). Alabastrine limestone, 39¾ x 22½
inches. Acc. no. 47.181. Gift of Mr. and Mrs. Leslie H. Green, 1947.

THE DRAGON OF BEL-MARDUK. From the Ishtar Gate, Babylon.
Reign of Nebuchadnezzar II (604-562 B.C.). Glazed tiles, 45½ x 65¾
inches. Acc. no. 31.25. Gift of the Founders Society, 1931.

SERVANT CARRYING A SKIN OF WINE. From the palace of Xerxes, Persepolis. Achaemenid Dynasty, reign of Xerxes I (485-465 B.C.). Limestone, 21½ x 11½ inches. Acc. no. 31.340. Gift of Mrs. Lillian Henkel Haass, 1931.

COURT OFFICIAL. Thirteenth Century. Polychromed stucco, 40 inches. Acc. no. 25.64. City appropriation, 1925.

COMBAT OF ARDASHIR AND ARDUWAN. Page from the Demotte Shah-Nameh. Mongol Dynasty, Fourteenth Century. Ink and tempera on paper, 16 x 11⅝ inches. Acc. no. 35.54. Gift of Edsel B. Ford, 1935.

LADY DAYDREAMING by Riza-i-Abbasi (about 1570-1640). Signed
and dated 1627. Tempera on paper, 9½ x 4¾ inches. Acc. no. 44.274.
Gift of Mrs. Edsel B. Ford, 1944.

MAITREYA. Northern Wei Dynasty (dated 520 A.D.). Gilt bronze, 17¾ inches. Acc. no. 30.303. Gift of Edsel B. Ford, 1930.

SAKYAMUNI AS AN ASCETIC. Yüan Dynasty (1279-1368 A.D.).
Lacquered wood, 11¾ inches. Acc. no. 29.172. City appropriation, 1929.

EARLY AUTUMN, *by Ch'ien Hsüan* (1235-1270 A.D.). Painting on paper, 10½ x 47¼ inches. Acc. no. 29.1. Gift of the Founders Society, 1929.

LANDSCAPE (DETAIL), *by Kuo Hsü* (1456-1526 A.D.). Ink on paper, 8½ x 62 inches. Acc. no. 42.51. Gift of the Sarah Bacon Hill Fund, 1942.

JIZO AS LORD OF PURGATORY. Korai Period (928-1392 A.D.).
Painting on silk, 86 x 128 inches. Acc. no. 24.106. City appropriation, 1924.

SPRING IN THE PALACE (DETAIL), *attributed to Tosa Mitsunori* (*1583-1638* A.D.). Color and gold on paper, 67 x 141 inches. Acc. no. 27.541. City appropriation, 1927.

UMA. Fourteenth-Fifteenth Century A.D. Copper, 40⅞ inches. Acc. no.
41.81. Gift of the Sarah Bacon Hill Fund, 1941.

GAURA MALLARA RAGINI (A HINDU MUSICAL MODE). *Rajasthani School* (about 1600 A.D.). Painting on paper, 7¾ x 5¾ inches. Acc. no. 26.388. Gift of the Founders Society, 1926.

GARUDA. Reign of Suryavarman II (1112-1152 A.D.). Bronze, 9¾ inches. Acc. No. 43.419. Gift of Albert Kahn, 1943.

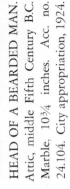

HEAD OF A BEARDED MAN. Attic, middle Fifth Century B.C. Marble, 10¾ inches. Acc. no. 24.104. City appropriation, 1924.

HEAD OF A BEARDED MAN. Cypriote, Sixth Century B. C. Limestone, 12½ inches. Acc. no. 24.105. City appropriation, 1924.

DRAPED STANDING FIGURE OF A WOMAN. Attic, Fourth Century
B.C. Marble, 61 inches. Acc. no. 24.113. City appropriation, 1924.

DRAPED KNEELING FIGURE OF A WOMAN. Attic, Fifth Century
B.C. Marble, 20¾ inches. Acc. no. 22.207. Gift of Ralph Harman Booth,
1924.

GODDESS OF A CITY, OR CYBELE. Fourth Century B.C. Marble, 20½ inches. Acc. no. 41.9. Gift of the Founders Society, 1941.

RIDER. Second half Fifth Century B.C. Bronze, 10½ inches. Acc. no. 46.260. City appropriation, 1946.

HEAD OF AUGUSTUS. Emperor, 31 B.C.-14 A.D. Marble, 19 inches. Acc. no. 24.101. Gift of Mr. and Mrs. James S. Holden, 1927.

HEAD OF A MAN. First Century B.C. Marble, 16 inches. Acc. no. 27.211. City appropriation, 1927.

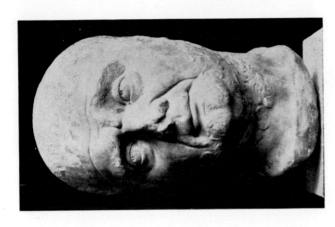

HEAD OF PHILIPPUS ARABS. Emperor, 244-249 A.D. Marble, 12½ inches. Acc. no. 27.212. Gift of Mr. and Mrs. James S. Holden, 1927.

HEAD OF A BEARDED MAN. Reign of Septimius Severus (193-212 A.D.). Marble, 10½ inches. Acc. no. 27.222. Gift of Mr. and Mrs. James S. Holden, 1927.

OSCILLUM OR ROTATING MEDALLION WITH RELIEFS OF A SATYR AND A MAENAD. Neo-Attic Style, First Century B.C. Marble, diameter 16⅞ inches. Acc. no. 45.130. City appropriation, 1945.

SARCOPHAGUS: WINGED VICTORIES AND EROTES WITH GARLANDS.
Second Century A.D. Marble, 27 x 73½ inches. Acc. no. 27.208. City appropriation, 1927.

SARCOPHAGUS: ORANT WOMAN, CHRIST AS ORATOR, GOOD SHEPHERD.
Early Christian, Third Century A.D. Marble, 25½ x 85½ inches. Acc. no. 26.138.
City appropriation, 1926.

STANDING BULL. Late First Century B.C.—early First Century A.D. Bronze, 6¾ inches. Acc. no. 45.120. City appropriation, 1945.

PERSONIFICATION OF THE RIVER TIGRIS. From Seleucia Pieria, Syria. Second or Third Century A.D. Mosaic of stone tesserae, 56¾ x 56¼ inches. Acc. no. 40.127. City appropriation, 1940.

HEAD OF VALENTINIAN I. Emperor, 364-375 A.D. Marble, 4 inches.
Acc. no. 37.157. Gift of Dr. W. R. Valentiner, 1937.

MUMMY PORTRAIT OF A WOMAN. From the Fayum. Roman Period, Second-Third Century A.D. Wax encaustic on panel, 17½ x 9¾ inches. Acc. no. 25.2. Gift of Julius H. Haass, 1925.

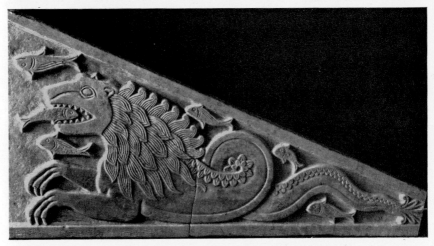

TWO RELIEFS FROM THE PARAPET OF A PULPIT. Italo-Byzantine, probably late Ninth or early Tenth Century. Marble, 20¼ x 42¼ and 20¼ x 41½ inches. Acc. nos. 43.447 and 43.448. Gift of the Founders Society, 1943.

ST. GRISANTIUS. North Italy (Reggio), early Thirteenth Century.
Marble, 28¾ x 24¼ inches. Acc. no. 22.145. Gift of J. G. Demotte, 1922.

CRUCIFIX. Tuscany, late Thirteenth Century. Polychromed wood, 80 x 55 inches. Acc. no. 27.584. Gift of Elia Volpi, 1927.

MADONNA AND CHILD ENTHRONED. Tuscany, Thirteenth Century.
Polychromed wood, 62½ inches. Acc. no. 30.383. Gift of Mr. and Mrs.
Edsel B. Ford, 1930.

CRUCIFIXION *by Turone, Verona* (*fl. third quarter of Fourteenth Century*). Panel, 58½ x 21¼ inches. Acc. no. 38.25. City appropriation, 1938.

TRIPTYCH: MADONNA ENTHRONED; NATIVITY; CRUCI-
FIXION *by Allegretto Nuzi,* Fabriano (*fl. 1350-74*). Panel, 18⅝ x 8¾
inches. Gift of James E. Scripps, 1889.

CRUCIFIXION *by the Master of the St. George Codex,* Siena (*fl. 1330-50*). Panel, 18½ x 9⅞ inches. Acc. no. 36.75. Gift of the George L. Hull Fund, 1936.

MADONNA AND CHILD *by Tino da Camaino,* Siena and Naples (*about 1285-1339*). Marble, 19¼ inches. Acc. no. 25.147. City appropriation, 1925.

MADONNA AND CHILD *by Andrea Pisano,* Pisa *(about 1270-1348).*
Marble, 30 inches. Acc no. 27.160. Gift of Mr. and Mrs. Edsel B. Ford,
1927.

MADONNA AND CHILD WITH ANGELS *by Agostino di Giovanni,*
Siena (*1285/90-1348*). Marble, 30 x 37 inches. Acc. no. 25.151. City
appropriation, 1925.

THE TRINITY *by Masolino,* Florence *(1383-1447).* Panel, 65 x 34½ inches. Acc. no. 25.145. City appropriation, 1925.

THE MOURNING ST. JOHN *by Andrea del Castagno* (?), Florence (*1423-1457*). Panel, 46¾ x 17⅝ inches. Acc. no. 37.37. Gift of Edsel B. Ford, 1937.

THE BETRAYAL OF CHRIST *by Sassetta*, Siena (*1392-1450*). Panel, 14⅞ x 23⅜ inches. Acc. no. 46.56. City appropriation, 1946.

THE PROCESSION TO CALVARY *by Sassetta*, Siena (*1392-1450*).
Panel, 19¼ x 25 inches. Acc. no. 24.94. City appropriation, 1924.

MADONNA AND CHILD *by Luca della Robbia,* Florence (*1400-1481*). Glazed terra cotta, 19¾ x 15¼ inches. Acc. no. 29.355. City appropriation, 1929.

MADONNA AND CHILD *by Andrea della Robbia,* Florence (*1435-1525*). Glazed terra cotta, 47¼x29⅜ inches. Acc. no. 45.514. Gift of Mr. and Mrs. Walter O. Briggs, 1945.

MADONNA AND CHILD *by Lorenzo Ghiberti,* Florence *(1378-1455).*
Polychromed terra cotta, 27 inches. Acc. no. 40.79. Gift of the Ralph Harman Booth Fund, 1940.

COAT-OF-ARMS OF THE MINERBETTI FAMILY *by Donatello,* Florence (*1386-1466*). Sandstone, 85 x 29¼ inches. Acc. no. 41.124. Gift of Mr. and Mrs. Edsel B. Ford, 1941.

JUDITH *by Antonio Pollaiuolo,* Florence and Rome (*about 1432-1489*).
Bronze, 16⅞ inches. Acc. no. 37.147. Gift of Mrs. Edsel B. Ford, 1937.

PROFILE OF A YOUNG WOMAN *by Desiderio da Settignano,* Florence
(*1428-1464*). Stone (pietra serena), 20¼ x 13 inches. Acc. no. 48.152.
Gift of Mrs. Edsel B. Ford in memory of her husband, 1948.

THE THREE ARCHANGELS WITH TOBIAS *by Neri di Bicci,* Florence
(*1419-1491*). Panel, 71 x 68¾ inches. Acc. no. 26.114. City appropriation, 1926.

THE DEPOSITION OF CHRIST *by Carlo Crivelli,* Venice (*about 1430-1495*). Panel, 16½ x 45 inches. Acc. no. 25.35. Gift of the Founders Society, 1925.

THE RESURRECTED CHRIST *by Sandro Botticelli,* Florence (*1444-1510*). Panel, 18 x 11¾ inches. Acc. no. 27.3. Gift of Dr. W. R. Valentiner, 1927.

PORTRAIT OF AN OLD MAN *by Domenico Ghirlandajo,* Florence
(*1449-1494*). Fresco, 20 x 14⅝ inches. Acc. no. 31.53. Gift of the
Founders Society, 1931.

CHRIST AT THE COLUMN *by Antonello da Messina,* South Italy and Venice (*about 1430-1479*). Wood transferred to canvas, 14½ x 11¾ inches. Acc. no. 34.192. Gift of the Ralph Harman Booth Fund, 1934.

PORTRAIT OF A LADY *by Andrea Verrocchio,* Florence (*1436-1488*) or *Leonardo da Vinci,* Florence and Milan (*1452-1519*). Panel, 14¼ x 10 inches. Acc. no. 36.90. Gift of the Founders Society, 1936.

ELEONORA DA TOLEDO AND HER SON, DON GARCIA *by Agnolo Bronzino,* Florence (*1503-1572*). Panel, 47½ x 39¼ inches. Acc. no. 42.57. Gift of Mrs. Ralph Harman Booth, in memory of her husband, 1942.

THE MYSTIC MARRIAGE OF ST. CATHERINE *by Correggio,* Parma
(*1494-1534*). Panel, 52 4/5 x 48 2/5 inches. Acc. no. 26.94. Gift of Mrs.
Anna Scripps Whitcomb as a memorial to James E. Scripps, 1926.

PORTRAIT OF AN ARTIST *by Franciabigio,* Florence (*1482-1525*).
Panel, 15½ x 11¾ inches. Acc. no. 89.7. Gift of James E. Scripps, 1889.

NOLI ME TANGERE *by Luca Signorelli,* Umbria *(about 1441-1523).*
Panel, 8 x 17½ inches. Acc. no. 29.41. City appropriation, 1929.

THE RESURRECTED CHRIST APPEARING TO HIS DISCIPLES *by
Luca Signorelli,* Umbria (about 1441-1523). Panel, 8 x 17½ inches. Acc.
no. 29.42. City appropriation, 1929.

MADONNA AND CHILD *by Giovanni Bellini,* Venice (*about 1431-1516*). Panel, 33⅜ x 41¾ inches. Acc. no. 28.115. City appropriation, 1928.

MADONNA AND CHILD *by Andrea Previtali*, Brescia (*1470-1528*).
Panel, 24 x 22½ inches. Acc. no. 22.8. City appropriation, 1922.

MADONNA AND CHILD *by Cima da Conegliano,* Venice (*about 1460-1517*). Panel, 25¾ x 19 inches. Acc. no. 89.11. Gift of James E. Scripps, 1889.

THE DRUNKENNESS OF NOAH *by Palma Vecchio,* Venice (*about 1480-1528*). Canvas, 26 x 60 inches. Acc. no. 26.305. Gift of Thomas Agnew and Sons, 1926.

THE SACRIFICE OF NOAH *by Palma Vecchio,* Venice (*about 1480-1528*). Canvas, 26 x 60 inches. Acc. no. 26.304. Gift of Thomas Agnew and Sons, 1926.

JUDITH WITH THE HEAD OF HOLOFERNES *by Titian,* Venice
(1477-1576). Canvas, 44½ x 37½ inches. Acc. no. 35.10. Gift of Edsel
B. Ford, 1935.

MAN WITH A FLUTE *by Titian,* Venice *(1477-1576).* Canvas, 38½ x 30 inches. Acc. no. 27.385. Gift of the Founders Society, 1927.

PORTRAIT OF A YOUNG MAN *by Giovanni Battista Moroni,* Bergamo (*about 1520-1578*). Canvas, 24 x 17½ inches. Acc. no. 29.244. Gift of Howard Young, 1929.

THE DREAMS OF MEN *by Tintoretto,* Venice *(1518-1594).* Canvas,
167¼ x 85⅜ inches. Acc. no. 23.11. City appropriation, 1923.

JUPITER *by Benvenuto Cellini,* Florence *(1500-1571).* Bronze, 11½ inches. Acc. no. 38.102. Gift of Mrs. Allan Shelden, 1938.

A NIOBID *by Francesco da Sant' Agata,* Padua (*fl. about 1520*). Bronze, 13½ inches. Acc. no. 37.148. Gift of Mrs. Edsel B. Ford, 1937.

ST. DANIEL OF PADUA AND ST. LOUIS OF TOULOUSE *by Bernardo Zenale,* Milan *(1436-1526)*. Panel, 25⅛ x 26 inches. Acc. no. 43.1. Gift of Mrs. Ralph Harman Booth in memory of her husband, 1943.

THE MYSTIC MARRIAGE OF ST. CATHERINE *by Paolo Veronese,*
Venice (*1528-1588*). Canvas, 66½ x 46 inches. Acc. no. 44.265. Gift of
Mr. and Mrs. Walter O. Briggs, 1944.

ALLEGORY OF AUTUMN *by Jacopo Sansovino,* Venice *(1486-1570).*
Terra cotta, 13 x 13¼ inches. Acc. no. 45.25. Gift of Mr. and Mrs. E.
Raymond Field, 1945.

PHILIP IV OF SPAIN *by Pietro Tacca,* Florence (*1580-1650*). Bronze,
15¾ inches. Acc. no. 29.348. City appropriation, 1929.

PORTRAIT OF FEDERICO, PRINCE OF URBINO, AT THE AGE OF
TWO YEARS *by Federico Baroccio,* Urbino (*1526-1612*). Canvas, 37¾
x 25½ inches. Acc. no. 44.216. Gift of Robert H. Tannahill, 1944.

HOLY FAMILY WITH ST. FRANCIS *by Annibale Carracci*, Bologna (*1560-1609*). Oil on copper, 18½ x 14½ inches. Acc. no. 46.280. Gift of Mr. and Mrs. E. Raymond Field, 1946.

ST. JEROME IN THE DESERT *by Pietro da Cortona,* Rome (*1596-1669*). Oil on copper, 17⅝ x 15¼ inches. Acc. no. 42.56. Gift of Mr. and Mrs. E. Raymond Field, 1942.

THE FRUIT VENDOR *by Caravaggio,* Rome *(1569-1610).* Canvas, 51¼ x 35½ inches. Acc. no. 36.10. Gift of Edsel B. Ford, 1936.

THE ADORATION OF THE SHEPHERDS *by Luca Giordano,* Naples (*1632-1705*). Canvas, 27⅝ x 20⅞ inches. Acc. no. 44.3. Gift of the Founders Society, 1944.

CHRIST AND THE WOMAN OF SAMARIA *by Guercino,* Bologna (*1591-1666*). Canvas, 39 x 54¼ inches. Acc. no. 26.108. City appropriation, 1926.

MADONNA AND CHILD WITH ADORING FIGURE *by Giovanni Battista Tiepolo,* Venice *(1696-1770).* Canvas, 74 x 57 inches. Acc. no. 38.56. Gift of Mr. and Mrs. Edsel B. Ford, 1938.

ALEXANDER THE GREAT WITH THE DAUGHTERS OF DARIUS
by Giovanni Battista Tiepolo, Venice *(1696-1770).* Canvas, 46¼ x 38½
inches. Acc. no. 25.207. Gift of the Founders Society, 1925.

ST. JOSEPH AND THE CHRIST CHILD *by Giovanni Battista Tiepolo,*
Venice *(1696-1770)*. Canvas, 60½ x 43¾ inches. Acc. no. 44.213. Gift
of Mr. and Mrs. Edgar B. Whitcomb, 1944.

VIEW OF THE TIBER WITH CASTEL SANT' ANGELO, ROME *by*
Bernardo Bellotto, Venice (*1720-1780*). Canvas, 34½ x 58½ inches. Acc.
no. 40.166. Gift of Mr. and Mrs. Edgar B. Whitcomb, 1940.

THE PIAZZA OF ST. MARK *by Canaletto*, Venice (1697-1768). Canvas,

ST. JEROME IN HIS STUDY *by Jan van Eyck* (*about 1390-1441*) and
Peter Christus (*about 1410-1472*). Panel, 8½ x 5¼ inches. Acc. no. 25.4.
City appropriation, 1925.

ST. JEROME IN THE DESERT *by Rogier van der Weyden (1399-1464)*.
Panel, 12⅛ x 9⅞ inches. Acc. no. 46.359. Gift of Mr. and Mrs. Edgar B.
Whitcomb, 1946.

THE VIRGIN IN THE ROSE GARDEN *by the Master of the St. Lucy Legend (active last quarter of the Fifteenth Century)*. Panel, 31⅛ x 23⅝ inches. Acc. no. 26.387. Gift of the Founders Society, 1926.

THE LAST JUDGMENT *by Jan Provost* (*1462-1529*). Panel, 22¾ x
23⅞ inches. Acc. no. 89.35. Gift of James E. Scripps, 1889.

THE ANNUNCIATION *by Gerard David (about 1450-1523)*. Panel,
13½ x 9 inches. Acc. no. 27.201. City appropriation, 1927.

ST. MARY MAGDALENE *by Quentin Massys* (*1466-1530*). Panel,
12 5/16 x 8⅞ inches. Acc. no. 40.130. Gift of the Sarah Bacon Hill Fund,
1940.

PORTRAIT OF A YOUNG MAN *by Barend van Orley (about 1492-1542)*. Panel, 5⅜ x 4¼ inches. Acc. no. 34.186. Gift of the Emma J. Farwell Fund, 1934.

ABBOT JOHANN INGENRAY *by Jan van Gossaert called Mabuse* (*about 1478- before 1536*). Dated 1535. Panel, 40 x 47 inches. Acc. no. 44.281. Gift of the Founders Society, 1944.

THE ADORATION OF THE MAGI *by Joos van Cleve (1485-1540?)*.
Center panel, 35 x 25½ inches; each wing, 35 x 11 inches. Acc. no. 45.420.
Gift of Mr. and Mrs. Edgar B. Whitcomb, 1945.

CATHERINE OF ARAGON AS THE MAGDALEN *by Master Michiel* (*Michel Sittow*) (*about 1469-1525*). Panel, 12⅝ x 9⅞ inches. Acc. no. 40.50. Gift of the Founders Society, 1940.

TWO COURT FOOLS *by Frans Floris* (*about 1516-1570*). Panel, 25½ x 21 inches. Acc. no. 39.1. Gift of the Founders Society, 1939.

THE WEDDING DANCE by Pieter Brueghel the Elder (1525/30-1569).
Panel, 47 x 62 inches. Acc. no. 30.374. City appropriation, 1930.

FLOWERS *by Jan Brueghel, the Elder* (*1568-1625*). Panel, 36½ x 29⅛ inches. Acc. no. 35.105. Gift of Mrs. Anna Scripps Whitcomb, 1935.

PHILIPPE RUBENS *by Peter Paul Rubens (1557-1640)*. Panel, 27 x 21¼ inches. Acc. no. 26.385. Gift of William E. Scripps as a memorial to his son, James E. Scripps II, 1926.

HYGEIA, GODDESS OF HEALTH *by Peter Paul Rubens* (1577-1640).
Panel, 41¾ x 29¼ inches. Acc. no. 44.266. Gift of Mr. and Mrs. Henry
Reichold, 1944.

ABIGAIL MEETING DAVID WITH PRESENTS *by Peter Paul Rubens* *(1577-1640)*. Canvas, 67 x 98 inches. Acc. no. 89.63. Gift of James E. Scripps, 1889.

ARCHDUKE FERDINAND *by Peter Paul Rubens* (1577-1640). Panel, 47½ x 36 inches. Acc. no. 47.58. Gift of the Ralph Harman Booth Fund, 1947.

MARCHESA SPINOLA *by Anthony van Dyck (1599-1641)*. Canvas, 42 x
32½ inches. Acc. no. 26.102. Gift of Ralph Harman Booth, 1926.

THE HOLY FAMILY WITH ST. ANNE *by Jacob Jordaens (1593-1678)*. Panel, 44⅛ x 37½ inches. Acc. no. 46.300. Gift of Mrs. Ralph Harman Booth, 1946.

THE LEGEND OF ST. CHRISTOPHER *attributed to Jan Joest van Calcar (1460-1515)*. Panel, 18½ x 14½ inches. Acc. no. 44.259. Gift of the Founders Society, 1944.

CRUCIFIXION *by Aelbert van Ouwater* (*fl. 1460-1495*). Panel, 56 9/16 x 40⅜ inches. Acc. no. 41.126. Gift of Mr. and Mrs. Edgar B. Whitcomb, 1941.

THE ADORATION OF THE KINGS *by Jacob Cornelisz (about 1470-1533)*. Panel, 51¾ x 38¾ inches. Acc. no. 44.74. Gift of the Ralph Harman Booth Fund, 1944.

THE CRUCIFIXION *by Jan van Scorel* (*1495-1562*). Panel, 15 x 13½ inches. Acc. no. 34.15. Gift of the Julius H. Haass Fund, 1934.

RIVER LANDSCAPE *by Hercules Seghers (1589-1645)*. Canvas, 15⅜ x 25 inches. Acc. no. 38.68. Gift of the Founders Society, 1938.

THE BARNYARD *by Melchior de Hondecoeter (1636-1695)*. Canvas, 44¼ x 50 inches. Acc. no. 45.16. Gift of Mr. and Mrs. Edgar B. Whitcomb, 1945.

SELF PORTRAIT OF THE ARTIST IN HIS STUDIO *by Frans van Mieris (1635-1681)*. Canvas, 35¾ x 30¼ inches. Acc. no. 38.29. Gift of Mrs. Anna Scripps Whitcomb, 1938.

PORTRAIT OF A WOMAN *by Frans Hals (1584-1666)*. Panel, 28½ x 21½ inches. Acc. no. 23.27. City appropriation, 1923.

STILL LIFE WITH A GOLD CUP *by Willem Kalf* (*1622-1693*). Canvas, 22¾ x 19¼ inches. Acc. no. 26.43. Gift of the Founders Society, 1926.

CHURCH INTERIOR *by Emanuel de Witte (1617-1692)*. Canvas, 48 x
40½ inches. Acc. no. 37.1. City appropriation, 1937.

ITALIAN PEASANTS AND RUINS *by Jan Baptist Weenix* (*1621-1660*). Canvas, 26¼ x 31½ inches. Acc. no. 41.57. Gift of Mrs. John A. Bryant in memory of her husband, 1941.

MOTHER NURSING HER CHILD *by Pieter de Hooch* (*1628-about 1684*). Canvas, 31½ x 23½ inches. Acc. no. 89.39. Gift of James E. Scripps, 1889.

THE CEMETERY *by Jacob van Ruisdael (1628-1682)*. Canvas, 56 x 74½ inches. Acc. no. 26.3. Gift of Julius H. Haass in memory of his brother, Dr. E. W. Haass, 1925.

THE FAIR AT OEGSTGEEST *by Jan Steen* (*about 1626-1679*). Canvas, 28 x 39 inches. Acc. no. 39.673. Gift of Mr. and Mrs. Edgar B. Whitcomb, 1939.

THE WINDY DAY *by Jan van Goyen (1596-1656)*. Panel, 18 x 26
inches. Acc. no. 39.5. Gift of the Founders Society, 1939.

CANAL SCENE *by Salomon van Ruysdael (about 1600-1670)*. Canvas, 39 x 53¾ inches. Acc. no. 89.43. Gift of James E. Scripps, 1889.

LANDSCAPE WITH CATTLE *by Aelbert Cuyp* (*1620-1691*). Canvas,
39¾ x 52¾ inches. Acc. no. 89.33. Gift of James E. Scripps, 1889.

VIEW OF THE OUDE KIRK, DELFT *by Jan van der Heyden (1637-1712)*. Panel, 21¾ x 27⅞ inches. Acc. no. 48.218. Gift of Mr. and Mrs. B. Whitcomb, 1948.

HEAD OF BEARDED OLD MAN *by Rembrandt* (1606-1669). Panel, 21⅞ x 15¾ inches. Acc. no. 42.151. Gift of Mrs. Ellen Stevens Whitall, Mrs. Annie Stevens Woodruff and Mr. William P. Stevens, in memory of Henry G. Stevens, 1942.

HEAD OF CHRIST *by Rembrandt* (*1606-1669*). Panel, 10 x 9 inches. Acc. no. 30.370. Gift of the Founders Society, 1930.

THE VISITATION *by Rembrandt* (*1606-1669*). Panel, 22¼ x 18⅞ inches. Acc. no. 27.200. City appropriation, 1927.

MAN READING A LETTER *by Gerard Terborch* (*1617-1681*). Panel,
15 x 12¾ inches. Acc. no. 29.256. City appropriation, 1929.

SELF PORTRAIT *by Vincent van Gogh* (*1853-1890*). Canvas on wood, 13¾ x 10½ inches. Acc. no. 22.13. City appropriation, 1922.

THE ADORATION OF THE MAGI AND SAINTS. School of Cologne, about 1410. Center panel, 31¾ x 19 inches; each wing, 31¾ x 9½ inches. Acc. no 26.106. City appropriation, 1926.

PORTRAIT OF A YOUNG MAN *by Michael Wolgemut (1434-1519).*
Panel, 13⅛ x 9¼ inches. Acc. no. 41.1. Gift of Mr. and Mrs. Ernest
Kanzler in memory of Dr. and Mrs. Karl Kanzler, 1941.

THE CRUCIFIXION *by the Master of the Augsburg Visitation* (*fl. 1475*). Panel, 74½ x 41 inches. Acc. no. 22.146. Gift of Ralph Harman Booth, 1922.

ST. JOHN *by Jörg Lederer* (*about 1475-1550*). Polychromed wood, 52¾ inches. Acc. no. 26.14. Gift of Ralph Harman Booth, 1926.

MOURNING VIRGIN *by Jörg Lederer (about 1475-1550)*. Polychromed
wood, 53 inches. Acc. no. 43.3. Gift of Mrs. Ralph Harman Booth in
memory of her husband, 1943.

VIRGIN AND CHILD *by Jörg Syrlin the Younger (fl. 1480-1520)*. Poly-chromed wood, 39½ inches. Acc. no. 22.205. City appropriation, 1922.

VIRGIN AND CHILD *by Gregor Erhardt* (*fl. 1500*). Wood, 64 inches. Acc. no. 22.3. Gift of Ralph Harman Booth, 1922.

SIR HENRY GUILDFORD *by Hans Holbein the Younger* (*1497-1543*).
Panel, diameter 4¼ inches. Acc. no. 26.290. City appropriation, 1926.

PIETA *by Lucas Cranach the Elder (1472-1553)*. Panel, 29¼ x 38¼ inches. Acc. no. 36.1. Gift of Mrs. Lillian Henkel Haass and Walter F. Haass in memory of Reverend Charles W. F. Haass, 1936.

DRAPED FEMALE FIGURE *by Wilhelm Lehmbruck* (*1881-1919*).
Terra cotta, 19¾ inches. Acc. no. 29.347. City appropriation, 1929.

ASSUNTA *by George Kolbe* (*1877-1947*). Bronze, 76 inches. Acc. no.
29.331. City appropriation, 1929.

SEATED NUDE *by Gerhard Marcks* (1889-   ). Bronze, 20½ inches.
Acc. no. 44.270. Gift of Robert H. Tannahill, 1944.

RAIN CLOUDS, LAGO DI GARDA *by Karl Schmidt-Rottluff* (1884-).
Canvas, 34½ x 44¼ inches. Acc. no. 37.2. Gift of Mr. and Mrs. Henry
Reichhold, 1937.

VIEW OF JERUSALEM *by Oskar Kokoschka (1886-   )*. Canvas, 31½ x
50½ inches. Acc. no. 35.110. Gift of the Founders Society, 1935.

ST. GEORGE AND THE DRAGON. *School of Novgorod,* Fifteenth Century. Panel, 25½ x 19¼ inches. Acc. no. 38.69. William H. Murphy and Laura H. Murphy Funds, 1938.

CRUCIFIX. *Southern French School,* Twelfth Century. Polychromed wood, 94 x 61 inches. Acc. no. 28.3. Gift of Mrs. C. F. W. Haass in memory of her son, Dr. Ernest W. Haass, 1928.

APOSTLE. *School of Provence,* Twelfth Century. Limestone, 36½ inches.
Acc. no. 35.1. Gift of the Founders Society, 1935.

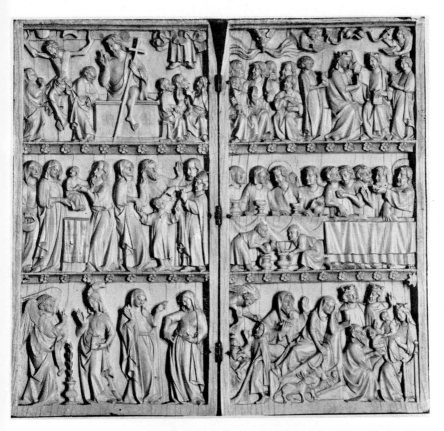

SCENES FROM THE LIFE OF CHRIST AND THE VIRGIN. First half
of the Fourteenth Century. Ivory, 9 13/16 x 10⅜ inches. Acc. no. 40.165.
Gift of Robert H. Tannahill, 1940.

VIRGIN AND CHILD, *School of Ile-de-France* (*St. Denis*), first half of the Fourteenth Century. Marble, 40 inches. Acc. no. 40.1. Gift of the Ralph Harman Booth Fund, 1940.

VIRGIN AND CHILD. *Workshop of Claus Sluter,* early Fifteenth Century. Stone, 41½ inches. Acc. no. 36.27. Gift of Mr. and Mrs. Edgar B. Whitcomb, 1936.

ST. ROBERT OF MOLESMES *by Enguerrand Quarton (about 1408-
after 1443).* Panel, 24 x 13 inches. Acc. no. 46.299. Gift of Mrs. Lillian
Henkel Haass, 1946.

ST. SEBASTIAN NURSED BY ST. IRENE *by Georges de la Tour (1593-1652)*. Canvas, 42¾ x 48¾ inches. Acc. no. 48.278. Gift of the Ralph Harman Booth Fund, 1948.

EVENING *by Claude Lorrain* (*1600-1682*). Canvas, 30¾ x 45½ inches. Acc. no. 41.10. Gift of Edsel B. Ford, 1941.

THE VILLAGE PIPER *by Antoine Le Nain* (*1588-1648*). Copper, 8½
x 11 9/16 inches. Acc. no. 30.230. City appropriation, 1930.

SELENE AND ENDYMION *by Nicolas Poussin* (*1594-1665*). Canvas, 48 x 66½ inches. Acc. no. 36.11. Gift of the Founders Society, 1936.

THE LAST SUPPER *by Philippe de Champaigne (1602-1674)*. Canvas, 43½ x 62¾ inches. Acc. no. 26.106. Gift of Ralph Harman Booth, 1926.

ST. LUIGI GONZAGA IN GLORY *by Pierre Legros II (1666-1719)*.
Terra cotta, 34 x 16 inches. Acc. no. 42.52. City appropriation, 1942.

LOUIS XIV *by François Girardon (1628-1715)*. Bronze, 42½ inches. Acc. no. 25.10. Gift of Julius Goldschmidt, 1925.

THE REPAST OF THE HUNTING PARTY *by Nicolas Lancret (1690-1745)*. Canvas, 22 x 29 inches. Acc. no. 28.95. City appropriation, 1928.

THE SHEPHERDESS OF THE ALPS *by Etienne Aubry* (*1745-1781*).
Canvas, 20 x 24½ inches. Acc. no. 48.12. Gift of Mr. and Mrs. Edgar
B. Whitcomb, 1948.

PORTRAIT OF CARDINAL DE FLEURY (1653-1743) *by Hyacinthe Rigaud (1659-1743)*. Canvas, 32 x 25¼ inches. Acc. no. 43.55. Gift of Mr. and Mrs. Ernest Kanzler, 1943.

MADAME HENRIETTE DE FRANCE AS A VESTAL VIRGIN *by Jean Marc Nattier (1685-1766)*. Canvas, 71 x 52½ inches. Acc. no. 43.417. Gift of Mr. and Mrs. Edgar B. Whitcomb, 1943.

THE BIRTH OF VENUS *by François Boucher* (*1703-1770*). Canvas, 69 x 30¼ inches. Acc. no. 29.445. Gift of Mr. and Mrs. Edgar B. Whitcomb, 1929.

ROMAN YOUTH WITH HORSE *by Jacques-Louis David* (*1748-1825*).
Canvas, 36¼ x 29¾ inches. Acc. no. 27.245. Gift of Mr. and Mrs. Edgar
B. Whitcomb, 1927.

PORTRAIT OF AN ARTIST *by Théodore Géricault* (*1791-1824*). Canvas, 29¼ x 23⅜ inches. Acc. no. 30.274. City appropriation, 1930.

MIDDAY DREAM *by Gustave Courbet* (*1819-1877*). Canvas, 32 x 25½ inches. Acc. no. 29.202. City appropriation, 1929.

THE MILLS OF DORDRECHT *by Charles François Daubigny (1817-1878).* Canvas, 33½ x 57½ inches. Acc. no. 32.85. Gift of Mr. and Mrs. E. Raymond Field, 1932.

GLADIOLAS *by Claude Monet (1840-1926)*. Canvas, 23½ x 32 inches.
Acc. no. 21.71. City appropriation, 1921.

CHURCH AT MORET AFTER THE RAIN *by Alfred Sisley (1840-1899)*. Canvas, 28¾ x 23¾ inches. Acc. no. 20.114. City appropriation, 1920.

GRAZIELLA *by Pierre-Auguste Renoir (1841-1919)*. Canvas, 25¾ x 21¼ inches. Acc. no. 20.111. City appropriation, 1920.

MADEMOISELLE BIANCHINI *by Charles Despiau* (1874-   ). Bronze,
15 inches. Acc. no. 35.7. Gift of the Founders Society, 1935.

THE GREEN ROOM *by Edgar Degas (1834-1917)*. Canvas, 16¼ x 34½ inches. Acc. no. 21.5. City appropriation, 1921.

THE WINDOW *by Henri Matisse* (*1869-*   ). Canvas, 57½ x 46 inches. Acc. no. 22.14. City appropriation, 1922.

ST. FRANCIS IN ECSTASY *by El Greco* (*1547-1614*). Canvas, 42¼ x
32 inches. Acc. no. 31.279. Gift of Mr. and Mrs. Edgar B. Whitcomb, 1931.

THE FLIGHT INTO EGYPT *by Bartolomé Esteban Murillo (1617-1682).*
Canvas, 81¾ x 61½ inches. Acc. no 48.96. Gift of Mr. and Mrs. K. T.
Keller, Mr. and Mrs. Leslie H. Green and Mr. and Mrs. Robert N. Green,
1948.

PORTRAIT OF A MAN *by Diego Velásquez (1599-1660)*. Canvas, 20¼ x 15¾ inches. Acc. no. 29.264. Gift of the Founders Society, 1929.

BUST OF AN OLD MAN *by Jusepe de Ribera (1588-1652)*. Canvas, 21½ x 19 inches. Acc. no. 89.72. Gift of James E. Scripps, 1889.

PORTRAIT OF THE COUNTESS DE GONDOMAR *by Francisco Goya*
(*1746-1828*). Canvas, 34⅜ x 25¾ inches. Acc. no. 41.80. Gift of the
Ralph Harman Booth Fund, 1941.

PORTRAIT OF A LADY *by William Hogarth* (*1697-1764*). Canvas, 29¾ x 25¼ inches. Acc. no. 27.11. Gift of the Founders Society, 1927.

PORTRAIT OF A YOUNG WOMAN *by Joseph Highmore* (*1692-1780*). Canvas, 18¼ x 14¼ inches. Acc. no. 25.221. Gift of Mrs. John S. Newberry, 1925.

HENRY DAVID ERSKINE, TWELFTH EARL OF BUCHAN *by Sir Henry Raeburn (1756-1823)*. Canvas, 50 x 48 inches. Acc. no. 20.100. City appropriation, 1920.

HIGH TOR OF MATTOCK BY MOONLIGHT *by Joseph Wright* (*1734-1797*). Canvas, 25 x 30 inches. Acc. no. 48.4. Gift of the Founders Society, 1948.

THE WILKINSON FAMILY *by Benjamin Wilson* (*1721-1788*). Canvas, 40¼ x 50⅜. Acc. no. 46.133. Gift of the Founders Society, 1946.

LOVE IN A VILLAGE *by John Zoffany (1733-1810)*. Canvas, 40 x 50 inches. Acc. no. 47.398. Gift of Mr. and Mrs. Edgar B. Whitcomb, 1947.

PORTRAIT OF AN ARTIST *by Matthew Pratt (1734-1805)*. Canvas,
30 x 25 inches. Acc. no. 38.14. Gift of Dexter M. Ferry, Jr., 1938.

BACCHUS AND ARIADNE *by Gustavus Hesselius (1682-1755)*. Canvas, 24½ x 32⅜ inches. Acc. no. 48.1. Gift of Dexter M. Ferry, Jr., 1948.

MRS. JOSIAH MARTIN *by Robert Feke (1705-1750)*. Canvas, 50½ x
40½ inches. Acc. no. 44.283. Gift of Dexter M. Ferry, Jr., 1944.

LUCY BRADLEY *by Ralph Earl* (*1751-1801*). Canvas, 44⅛ x 31 5/16 inches. Acc. no. 41.4. Gift of Dexter M. Ferry, Jr., 1941.

JOHN GRAY *by John Singleton Copley (1737-1815)*. Canvas, 49 7/16 x 39 5/16 inches. Acc. no. 43.30. Gift of the Gibbs-Williams Fund, 1943.

WATSON AND THE SHARK *by John Singleton Copley (1737-1815)*.
Canvas, 36 x 30½. Acc. no. 46.310. Gift of Dexter M. Ferry, Jr., 1946.

COLONEL JOHN MONTRESOR *by John Singleton Copley* (*1737-1815*). Canvas, 30 x 25 inches. Acc. no. 41.37. Gift of the Gibbs-Williams Fund, 1941.

JOHN TRUMBULL, POET AND COUSIN OF THE ARTIST *by John Trumbull (1756-1843)*. Canvas, 30 x 24 inches. Acc. no. 38.13. Gift of Dexter M. Ferry, Jr., 1938.

GENERAL WILLIAM NORTH *by Charles Willson Peale (1741-1827)*.
Canvas, 23 x 19 inches. Acc. no. 42.117. Gift of Dexter M. Ferry, Jr., 1942.

GENERAL AMASA DAVIS *by Gilbert Stuart (1755-1828)*. Panel, 32¾ x 26¼ inches. Acc. no. 45.17. Gift of Mrs. J. Bell Moran, 1945.

SELF PORTRAIT *by Rembrandt Peale (1778-1860)*. Canvas, 19 x 14¼ inches. Acc. no. 45.469. Gift of Dexter M. Ferry, Jr., 1945.

JACOB HOUSEMAN *by John Wesley Jarvis (1780-1839)*. Panel, 34 x 26½ inches. Acc. no. 41.55. Gift of Dexter M. Ferry, Jr., 1941.

THE FLIGHT OF FLORIMELL *by Washington Allston* (*1779-1843*).
Canvas, 35¾ x 28½ inches. Acc. no. 44.165. City appropriation, 1944.

IN NATURE'S WONDERLAND *by Thomas Doughty* (1793-1856).
Canvas, 24¼ x 30 inches. Acc. no. 35.119. Gift of the Gibbs-Williams
Fund, 1935.

THE LADY FROM HORNELL. *American School (New York State) (1810-1820)*. Panel, 23¾ x 25¾ inches. Acc. no. 36.91. Gift of the Gibbs-Williams Fund, 1936.

DR. AND MRS. EDWARD HUDSON *by Thomas Sully* (1783-1872). Canvas, each 29 x 23¾ inches. Acc. no. 26.89 and 26.90. City appropriation, 1926.

BANJO PLAYER *by William S. Mount* *(1807-1868)*. Canvas, 25 x 30 inches. Acc. no. 38.60. Gift of Dexter M. Ferry, Jr., 1938.

CASCADE IN THE FOREST *by John Frederick Kensett (1818-1872)*.
Canvas, 29½ x 26 inches. Acc. no. 27.598. Gift of Guy P. Turnbull, 1927.

IN THE FIELDS *by Eastman Johnson (1824-1906)*. Academy Board, 17¾ x 27½ inches. Acc. no. 38.1. Gift of Dexter M. Ferry, Jr., 1938.

LANDSCAPE ON THE RHINE *by Thomas Worthington Whittredge*
(1820-1910). Canvas, 27 x 35¾ inches. Acc. no. 45.468. Gift of D. M.
Ferry, Jr, 1945.

APPLE ORCHARD *by George Inness (1825-1894)*. Canvas, 30 x 45⅛ inches. Acc. no. 23.100. Presented in memory of Henry Brockholst Ledyard by his children, Baroness von Ketteler, Henry Ledyard and Hugh Ledyard, 1923.

VIEW OF RUTLAND, VERMONT *by Asher B. Durand* (*1796-1856*)
Canvas, 29⅛ x 42⅛ inches. Acc. no. 42.59. Gift of Dexter M. Ferry, Jr.,
1942.

SELF PORTRAIT *by William Page* *(1810-1885)*. Canvas, 59 x 36 inches.
Acc. no. 37.60. Gift of Mr. and Mrs. George S. Page, Mr. Blinn S. Page,
Mr. Lowell Briggs Page, and Miss Lesslie Stockton Howell, 1937.

THE DINNER HORN *by Winslow Homer* (1836-1910). Canvas, 11⅛ x 14¼ inches. Acc. no. 47.81. Gift of Dexter M. Ferry, Jr., 1947.

GIRL AND LAUREL *by Winslow Homer* (*1836-1910*). Canvas, 22⅝ x 15¾ inches. Acc. no. 40.56. Gift of Dexter M. Ferry, Jr., 1940.

ROBERT M. LINDSAY ("THE PRINT COLLECTOR") *by Thomas Eakins (1844-1916)*. Canvas, 24 x 20 inches. Gift of Dexter M. Ferry, Jr., 1935.

NOCTURNE IN BLACK AND GOLD: THE FALLING ROCKET *by James Abbott McNeill Whistler (1834-1903)*. Panel, 23¾ x 18⅜ inches. Acc. no. 46.309. Gift of Dexter M. Ferry, Jr., 1946.

SELF PORTRAIT *by James Abbott McNeill Whistler (1834-1903)*. Canvas, 29½ x 21 inches. Acc. no. 34.27. Bequest of Henry Glover Stephens, in memory of Ellen P. Stevens and Mary M. Stevens, 1934.

PORTRAIT OF A WOMAN *by William M. Chase (1849-1916)*. Canvas,
72 x 36 inches. Acc. no. 43.486. Gift of Henry Munroe Campbell, 1943.

THE FENCING MASTER *by Gari Melchers (1860-1932)*. Canvas, 81¼ x 39½ inches. Acc. no. 13.9. Gift of Edward Chandler Walker, 1913.

WOMEN ADMIRING A CHILD *by Mary Cassatt* (*1855-1926*). Pastel, 26 x 32 inches. Acc. no. 08.8. Gift of Edward Chandler Walker, 1908.

EARLY MORNING *by Albert P. Ryder (1847-1917).* Panel, 11⅛ x
15⅞ inches. Acc. no. 34.9. Gift of Dexter M. Ferry, Jr., 1934.

A DAY IN JUNE *by George Bellows* (*1882-1925*). Canvas, 42 x 48 inches. Acc. no. 17.17. City appropriation, 1917.

McSORLEY'S BAR *by John Sloan (1871-   )*. Canvas, 26 x 32 inches
Acc. no. 24.2. Gift of the Founders Society, 1924.

VISION ANTIQUE *by Arthur B. Davies (1862-1928)*. Canvas, 38 x 46 inches. Acc. no. 27.12. City appropriation, 1927.

EVENING *by John Carroll* (*1892-*   ). Fresco, 9½ x 18½ feet. Acc. no.
36.68. Gift of Mrs. Ernest Kanzler, 1936.

BASEMENT ROOM *by Charles Sheeler (1883-   )*. Canvas, 36 x 29 inches. Acc. no. 45.455. Gift of Robert H. Tannahill, 1945.

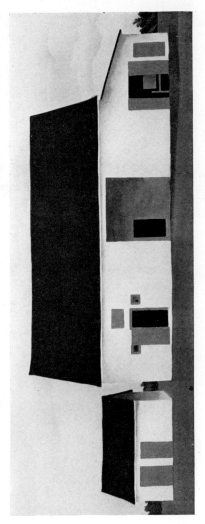

STABLES *by Georgia O'Keeffe* (1887-   ). Canvas, 12 x 32 inches. Acc. no. 45.454. Gift of Robert H. Tannahill, 1945.

FREIGHT CARS UNDER A BRIDGE *by Charles Burchfield* (1893-   ).
Watercolor, 24 x 34 inches. Acc. no. 34.25. Gift of Dr. George Kamperman, 1934.

LOG JAM, PENOBSCOT BAY *by Marsden Hartley (1817-1943)*. Canvas, 30½ x 40 15/16 inches. Acc. no. 44.5. Gift of Robert H. Tannahill, 1944.

SIDE WHEELER *by Lyonel Feininger* (*1871-*   ). Canvas, 31¾ x 39⅝ inches. Acc. no. 21.208. City appropriation, 1921.

SUMMER STORM *by Yasuo Kuniyoshi* (1893-   ). Canvas, 26 x 38¼
inches. Acc. no. 41.16. Gift of Dr. and Mrs. George Kamperman, 1941.

STILL LIFE *by Franklin Watkins* (1894-   ). Canvas, 37 x 51 inches.
Acc. no. 42.14. Merrill Fund, 1942.

GROTESQUE *by José Chavez Morado* (1909-   ). Panel, 24 x 30 inches.
Acc. no. 43.66. Gift of the Founders Society, 1943.

MEXICAN PUEBLO *by José Clemente Orozco* (*1883-*). Canvas, 30 x 37 inches. Acc. no. 42.103. Gift of the Founders Society, 1942.

DETROIT (DETAIL: THE MAKING OF A MOTOR) *by Diego Rivera* (1886-). Fresco. Acc. no. 33.10. Gift of Edsel B. Ford, 1933.